Words of Wisdom

JOHN F. KENNEDY

MENTOR
BOOKS

This Edition first published 2006 by

MENTOR BOOKS
43 Furze Road,
Sandyford Industrial Estate,
Dublin 18.
Tel. +353 1 295 2112   Fax. +353 1 295 2114
email: all@mentorbooks.ie
www.mentorbooks.ie

ISBN-10: 1-84210-344-X
ISBN-13: 978-1-84210-344-9

A catalogue record for this book
is available from the British Library

Designed and compiled by Nicola Sedgwick

1 3 5 7 9 10 8 6 4 2

Contents

Foreword

An icon of our times, John Fitzgerald Kennedy was born 29 May 1917 in Massachussetts, USA into the politically prominent Kennedy family. After an exemplary career in the military he entered politics and swiftly moved up the ranks of power. His youthful charm and charisma, along with high intellect and talent as a speaker, was an asset to his becoming the youngest person to be elected president in America. Major events during his presidency (January 1961 until his assassination in November 1963) included the Bay of Pigs invasion, the Cuban Missile Crisis, the building of the Berlin Wall, the Space Race, early events of the Vietnam War, and the American Civil Rights Movement.

Among the general public John F. Kennedy is often regarded as one of America's greatest presidents.

PUBLIC
SERVICE

*A*sk not
what your country
can do for you,
but what you can do
for your country.

Inaugural Address,
The Capitol, Washington DC
20 January 1961

★ ★ ★

*A*ll of us cannot
serve in our armed forces
or in the government,
but there is one thing
each of us can do,
and that is to take part
in our democracy,
to participate in it.

Statement urging citizens to vote
3 November 1962

★ ★ ★

*T*his is a free society . . .
and we do believe
that freedom and . . .
progress is best served by
permitting people to
advance their private interests
and the combination
of their great effort . . .
advances the public interest.

Remarks to Advertising Council
7 March 1962

EDUCATION

A country today
is only as strong as
its citizens are educated.

Address at the Jefferson Jackson dinner, Milwaulkee
12 May 1962

*A*ll of us
do not have equal talents,
but all of us
should have the opportunity
to develop these talents.

Commencement Address,
San Diego State College
6 June 1963

The human mind
is our fundamental resource.

Message to Congress on education
20 February 1961

POVERTY

*F*or the blessings of life have
not been distributed evenly
to the Family of Man.
[Therefore] the rich must help
the poor. The industrialised
nations must help the
developing nations.

Speech to Protestant Council
of City of New York
8 November 1963

23

*I*f a free society
cannot help the many
who are poor,
it cannot save the few
who are rich.

Inaugural Address,
The Capitol, Washington DC
20 January 1961

Young People

No nation can
neglect the development
of young people
without courting catastrophe.

Statement on youth employment
24 April 1963

*T*he future promise
of any nation
can be directly measured
by the present prospects
of its youth.

Message to Congress on the nation's youth
14 February 1963

SPIRITUALITY

★ ★ ★

*T*hough our convictions may
take us in many directions
in our faith, nevertheless
the basic presumption
of our moral law,
the existence of God,
man's relation to him –
there is general consensus
on these questions.

Remarks to National Conference
of Christians and Jews
21 November 1961

★ ★ ★

We have learned that
tolerance and cooperation
are ways to
true national strength.

Message given to American jewry
on Rosh Hashannah (Jewish New Year)
6 September 1961

*T*his country cannot afford
to be materially rich
and spiritually poor.

Annual Message to the Congress
on the State of the Union
January 14 1963

HEALTH

&

SOCIAL AFFAIRS

The manner in which
our nation cares for its citizens
and conserves its manpower
resources is more than
an index to its concern
for the less fortunate.
It is a key to its future.

Statement on a national program
to combat mental retardation
11 October 1961

*W*hat I think we are all
concerned about
is that children have
a happy childhood . . .
adults be permitted to work
and that older people find
their later years to be easier,
free from pain and discomfort.

Interview with Dave Garroway for *The Today Show*
31 January 1961

43

The health of our people
is our nation's most precious
resource.

Address marking opening
of Albert Einstein College of Medicine,
Bronx, New York
17 October 1955

44

EMPLOYMENT
&
BUSINESS

*W*e look upon man's toil
as an expression
of individual personality
and will,
not a commodity to be
exploited for the benefit of a
state or ruling political party.

Labour Day statement
29 August 1961

*L*et us never negotiate
out of fear.
But let us never fear
to negotiate.

Inaugural Address,
The Capitol, Washington DC, USA
20 January 1961

★ ★ ★

*T*he ideal of
full employment, in the large
sense that each individual shall
become all that he is capable
of becoming, and shall
contribute fully to the
wellbeing of the nation even
as he fully shares in that
wellbeing, is at the heart of
our democratic belief.

Message to Congress on manpower, 11 March 1963

★ ★ ★

THE ENVIRONMENT

★ ★ ★

*I*f we continue to ignore
the polluting of our streams,
the littering of our
national forests, we will be
denying to ourselves
and to our children
a heritage which we were
the beneficiaries of.

Campaign remarks, Valley Forge
19 October 1960

★ ★ ★

*W*e depend on natural
resources to sustain us –
but in turn their continued
availability must depend on
our using them prudently,
improving them wisely and,
where possible,
restoring them promptly.

Message to Congress on conservation
1 March 1962

★ ★ ★

*K*nowledge of the oceans
is more than a matter
of curiosity. Our very survival
depends on it . . .
to predict, and perhaps some
day to control, changes in
weather and climate
is of the utmost importance
to man everywhere.

Letter to Congress on oceanographic research
29 March 1963

EQUALITY

★ ★ ★

*A*nd no nation, large or small, can be indifferent to the fate of others, near or far. Modern economics, weaponry and communications have made us all realise more than ever that we are one human family and this one planet is our home.

Address before the Irish Parliament, Dublin, Ireland
28 June 1963

*W*e serve ourselves
and the stature of freedom
throughout the world
by serving our moral
commitment to equality.

Labor Day statement
29 August 1961

HUMAN
RIGHTS

*D*isagreement and dissent
are fundamental
to a free society.

Address to the Committee for Economic
Development
9 May 1963

*T*he right to vote
is very basic.
If we're going to neglect
that right,
then all of our talk
about freedom is hollow.

Press conference, State Department Auditorium,
Washington DC
13 September 1962

CULTURE

*W*e must never forget
that art is not
a form of propaganda;
it is a form of truth.

Amherst College, Massachusetts
October 26 1963

*I*f more politicians
knew poetry and more poets
knew politics,
I am convinced that the world
would be a little better place
to live.

Commencement Address at Harvard University,
Cambridge, Massachusetts
14 June 1956

*B*ehind the storm of
daily conflict and crisis . . .
the poet, the artist,
the musician continues
the quiet work of centuries,
building bridges of experience
between peoples, reminding
man . . . that the forces that
unite are deeper than those
that divide.

Remarks on behalf of the National Culture Centre,
National Guard Armory, Washington DC
29 November 1962

POLITICS

★ ★ ★

*W*e've learned that
you don't get far in politics
until you become
a total politician.
That means you've got to deal
with the party leaders
as well as the voters.
From now on, I'm going to be
a total politician.

Comments to advisors Kenneth O'Donnell
and David Powers, 1956

The men who create power
make an indispensable
contribution to
the nation's greatness,
but the men
who question power
make a contribution
just as indispensable.

Remarks at Amherst College, Massachusetts
26 October 1963

CONFLICT

*O*ur problems are
man-made,
therefore they may be solved
by man.
No problem of human destiny
is beyond human beings.

Address at the American University,
Washington DC
10 June 1963

Let both sides explore
what problems unite us
instead of belaboring
those problems
which divide us.

Inaugural Address,
The Capitol, Washington DC
20 January 1961

*M*ankind must put
an end to war,
or war will put an end
to mankind.

Address to the United Nations General Assembly,
New York
25 September 1961

PEACE

*W*herever we are,
we must all, in our daily lives,
live up to the age-old faith
that peace and freedom
walk together.

Commencement Address at the American University,
Washington DC
10 June 1963

*D*ay and night,
with every ounce of ingenuity
and industry we possess,
we must work for peace.
We must not have
another war.

Congressional campaign radio broadcast, 1946

★ ★ ★

This peace-keeping
machinery of the
United Nations cannot work
without the help of
the smaller nations . . .
Great powers have their
responsibilities, their burdens,
but the smaller nations
of the world must fulfil
their obligations as well.

Address to the Irish Parliament, Dublin, Ireland
28 June 1963

★ ★ ★

92

*W*hat kind of peace
do we seek? I am talking
about genuine peace,
the kind of peace that makes
life on earth worth living,
the kind that enables
men and nations to grow
and hope and build
a better life for their children.

Commencement Address at American University,
Washington DC
10 June 1963

FREEDOM

This is a small world and becoming smaller every day. The cause of freedom is under challenge all over the globe.

Remarks on the first C-141 all-jet transport
22 August 1963

Liberty is not easy to find.
It is a search that takes us
on a hard road.

Medal of Freedom presentation
21 February 1961

★ ★ ★

*Unless liberty flourishes
in all lands,
it cannot flourish in one . . .
For we live in an age
of interdependence
as well as independence –
an age of internationalism
as well as nationalism.*

At the Paulskirche, Frankfurt, Germany
25 June 1963

*B*ut however close
we sometimes seem
to that dark and final abyss,
let no man
of peace and freedom despair.
For he does not stand alone.

Address to the United Nations General Assembly,
New York
25 September 1961

COURAGE
& LEADERSHIP

★ ★ ★

*T*here are many kinds
of courage . . .
Perhaps the rarest courage
of all – for the skill to pursue
it is given to very few men –
is the courage to wage
a silent battle to illuminate
the nature of man and
the world in which he lives.

On the television program
Robert Frost: American Poet
26 February 1961

★ ★ ★

*T*hroughout history
those who live
in the most danger,
those who keep watch
at the gate,
are always prouder,
more courageous, more alive,
than those who live
far to the rear.

At Tegel Airport, Berlin, Germany
26 June 1963

*T*he only valid test
of leadership is the ability
to lead, and lead vigorously.

Democratic nomination acceptance speech,
Los Angeles
15 July 1960

*T*he times require leadership
which will stand against
the soft winds of indifference
and easy popularity
and personal gain.
They require leadership
which is disinterested,
responsible and dedicated.

Holyoke Trade High School, Holyoke, Massachusetts
June 1952

109

*L*eadership and learning
are indispensable
to each other.

Speech prepared for delivery in Dallas
the day of his assassination
22 November, 1963

SCIENCE

&

TECHNOLOGY

★ ★ ★

I think that if we could
increase the techniques
for improving education
in uneducated sections
of the world –
by using the latest devices of
science – that would be
an extraordinary
accomplishment . . .

Press conference, State Department Auditorium,
Washington DC
12 April 1961

113

★ ★ ★

*W*e choose
to go to the moon . . .
and do the other things,
not because they are easy,
but because they are hard,
because that goal will serve
to organise and measure
the best of our
energies and skills.

John F. Kennedy Moon Speech,
Rice University, Texas
12 September 1962

★ ★ ★

*B*ecause of the ingenuity
of science and man's
own inability to control
his relationships
one with another,
we happen to live
in the most dangerous time
in the history of
the human race.

Press conference, State Department Auditorium,
Washington DC
11 October 1961

★ ★ ★

*S*pace is open to us now,
and our eagerness
to share its meaning
is not governed by the efforts
of others.
We go into space because
whatever mankind
must undertake,
free men must fully share.

Message to Congress on urgent national needs
25 May 1961

THE
FUTURE

*Y*ou see things,
and you say 'Why?'
But I dream things
that never were,
and I say 'Why not?'

Address to the Irish Parliament, Dublin, Ireland,
quoting George Bernard Shaw
9 June 1963

★ ★ ★

This is not only the age
of the missile and
space vehicle and
thermonuclear power.
This is the age that can
become [humanity's] finest
hour in his search for
companionship
and understanding
and brotherhood.

Statement to the Association for Higher Education's
College and University Bulletin, 15 October 1960

Change is the law of life.
And those who look only
to the past or the present
are certain to miss
the future.

Address in the Assembly Hall at the Paulskirche,
Frankfurt, Germany
25 June 1963

A man may die,
nations may rise and fall,
but an idea lives on.

At the Franklin D. Roosevelt Birthplace
in Hyde Park, New York
14 August 1960

Photo Credits